PACIFIC NORTHWEST

MALLARD
PRESS

Photography
FPG
Odyssey Publishing

Photo Editor
Annette Lerner

MALLARD PRESS

An imprint of BDD Promotional
Book Company Inc.,
666 Fifth Avenue, New York,
NY 10103

Mallard Press and its
accompanying design and logo
are trademarks of BDD
Promotional Book Company, Inc.

Color separations by Advance
Laser Graphic Arts, Hong Kong.

Printed and bound in Hong Kong.

ISBN 0-7924-5488-X

*Previous pages: snow-laden trees
in deep midwinter close to the
summit of Mount Spokane,
eastern Washington, and (right)
cold sunshine silvering an open
stretch of ground in Wallowa-
Whitman National Forest,
northeastern Oregon.*

Where do you want to go for your next vacation? – the mountains or the seashore?

Choose the Pacific Northwest and you won't have to wrestle with the problem. The seascapes there are exciting, the mountain vistas dramatic and, in many parts of the Northwest, it is possible to experience both simply by turning your head.

The Pacific Northwest was first seen from the sea. Spanish explorers sailed past several times, but credit for its discovery goes to the English Captain James Cook, who charted its waters in 1778. He was looking for the fabled Northwest Passage, but his men made a discovery that, to them at least, was much more exciting. Local Indians gave them skins of the sea otter, which were perfect protection against the weather as they pushed on further north on their voyage of discovery. They were grateful for the warmth, but none of them knew what a treasure the skins really were until the following year when they put in at the port of Canton in China. One of the sailors was wearing a sea otter coat and when the Chinese saw it, they made him an offer he couldn't refuse. The coat was worth hundreds of dollars, as it turned out, so after his shipmates sold all the furs they had, they turned around and went back to North America for more. Before long, ships from Spain and Portugal, as well as England and the United States, were beating a path to the Pacific Northwest. By the beginning of the nineteenth century they were taking more than 10,000 sea otters a year, and measuring their profits from trips to China in hundreds of thousands of dollars.

Nonetheless, most people didn't really know what a treasure this territory was until the Lewis and Clark expedition reached the mouth of the Columbia River in 1805. By the time they made their way back to St. Louis the following summer, some Americans were already packing their bags for the long trip into the unknown that was called the Oregon Territory.

In 1811, John Jacob Astor sent men west to establish a fur trading post there, and a year later the British Navy arrived and took over. Oregon was a part of the British Empire for the next six years and home to missionaries and trappers and other hardy souls. American settlers began arriving in 1839 and, a few years later, wagon trains regularly rumbled along the Oregon Trail bringing thousands more in search of good agricultural land. What they found was some of the richest farmland on the continent. They also found wide-open pastures ideal for grazing and so, with cattle and sheep imported from California, they established ranches that are still flourishing.

Moreover they found lush forests, beginning there a timber industry that is still, after more than a hundred years of cutting, one of the most productive anywhere in the world. With thousands of miles of saltwater shoreline; even more thousands of miles of streams and rivers; and hundreds of lakes, fishing in general and salmon fishing in particular has become an industry worth hundreds of millions of dollars every year. The Columbia and other rivers provided a transportation route to get the bounty to the sea and on its way around the world. But they have also provided hydroelectric power and irrigation to make the farmland even more bountiful.

For all the change that civilization has brought, the Pacific Northwest is still one of America's great, unspoiled, natural wonders. Between them, Washington and Oregon have four national parks: exquisite Crater Lake; rugged and wild Olympic Mountains; majestic Mount Rainier, and glacier-filled North Cascades. More than a third of the land in both states is covered with forests.

Just about everyone who lives in the Northwest has a deep love of nature. Indeed, over recent years they have conducted campaigns to prevent outsiders from moving in from of fear that their paradise will become overcrowded. But tourism accounts for much of the state's wealth and it is a rare visitor who doesn't at least think about pulling up stakes and moving there permanently. Many do, but in Oregon, where there are about twenty-nine people per square mile, nearly sixty-eight percent live in urban areas; and in Washington, where the density is sixty-nine to the square mile, about seventy-four percent live in cities. That means there is still plenty of breathing space, and that, of course, is what attracts newcomers as well as visitors, and what makes all of them love the place. It takes your breath away at every turn.

Below: sunset on the beach of Harris Beach State Park reduces seabirds to silhouettes. Harris Beach lies on Highway 101, north of Brookings and is the most southerly of all Oregon's coast state parks. Its scenic rock cliffs along the ocean are one of its main attractions. Right: Shores Acres State Park, one of the loveliest state parks in Oregon. The park, which lies off Route 101 southwest of Coos Bay, was once the estate of Louis J. Simpson, son of the lumber baron Captain Asa M. Simpson. Failing in business, he gave all over to the state in 1934.

Crater Lake National Park (these pages) is Oregon's only national park; it came into being in 1902 after one William G. Steel spent nearly fifty years of his life lobbying Congress to act to preserve this unique lake. Situated on the crest of the Cascade Range in the caldera of an extinct volcano, the lake is six miles long and four-and-a-half miles wide. It is renowned for its clarity, its depth – it is the deepest lake in the country – and its intense color.

A midwinter view of a frozen Crater Lake, which, at almost 2,000 feet in depth, is the centerpiece of Crater Lake National Park, Oregon. The park is open all year round, though in years of very heavy snowfall, some roads fail to open by July.

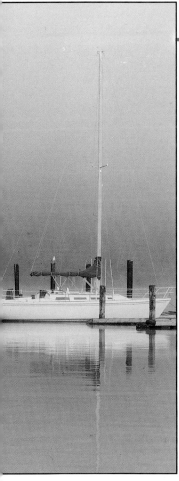

Above: mist rolls down over a quiet inlet on the Oregon coast and (left) fishing boats and pleasure craft tie up at Newport Harbor, where Oregon State University has established its Marine Science Center on Yaquina Bay. Right: Mount St. Helens, a peak that was devastated by a volcanic eruption in 1980. In May of that year over 150 square miles of timber were flattened and the popular recreational area of Spirit Lake was devastated by hurricane winds and tons of volcanic ash. Since then hiking trails have been cleared; now it is even possible to travel across the crater floor.

Above: Oregon's ice-encased summit of Mount Bachelor, which can be conquered the easy way via its summit chairlift (left). Mount Bachelor, which reaches a height of 9,000 feet, lies in the Cascade Range in central Oregon. The Cascades are comprised of fairly symmetrical volcanoes, of which Mount Bachelor is one. A mile-thick lava flow millions of years old still blankets the region, providing fertile soil for farmers, a legacy of the volcanic activity that created these mountains.

Left: a torrential waterfall on the slopes of Broken Top Mountain in the Cascade Range of central Oregon. The peak lies close to South Sister in the Three Sisters Wilderness, an area within Willamette National Forest, the most heavily timbered national forest in the country. Below: wave-rounded stones on the shore of Cape Arago State Park near Coos Bay, and (facing page) the Coquille River Lighthouse at Bullards Beach State Park in Bandon, both in Oregon. The light stands where river and ocean meet, an awkward spot reputedly known as a "navigator's nightmare."

Left: Silver Falls State Park, Oregon's largest state park, which covers 8,302 acres and can claim fourteen waterfalls, five of which are over a hundred feet in height. The park lies some twenty-five miles east of Salem, the state capital, where the State Capitol Building (below) was built in 1938. This modern marble edifice illustrates the state's early history in statuary– a twenty-four-foot-high statue of a bearded, axe-wielding pioneer tops the cylindrical dome, while marble sculptures on each side of the entrance depict the Lewis and Clark expedition and the covered wagons of those who pioneered the arduous Oregon Trail. Salem itself lies in the Willamette River Valley, midway between some of the finest mountain and coastal scenery in the world.

Above: "Portlandia," a gilded bronze statue by Raymond Kaskey decorating the Portland Building, an award-winning neo-classical design by Michael Graves in downtown Portland (remaining pictures), Oregon's largest city. Portland, which lies on the Willamette and Columbia rivers, once had a reputation as a sleepy place, but this is changing. Today it is internationally recognized for the quality of its architecture, its energy conservation programs and the beauty of its surroundings. The city began to develop as a settlement in the 1840s, becoming a major port during the 1870s, aided by the discovery of gold in Idaho and eastern Oregon. It is still an important port today, responsible for more wholesale trade than any other in the Pacific Northwest.

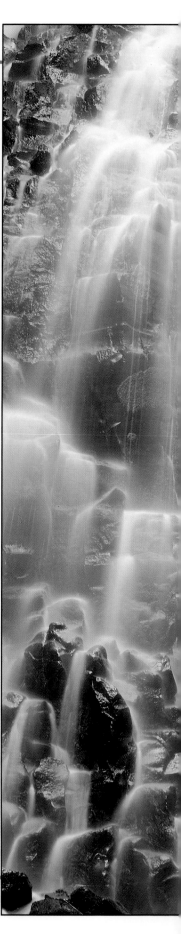

Mount Hood (above) has been called the monarch of the Oregon mountains. The Central Cascade Range boasts a number of lone peaks of distinctive appearance, but Mount Hood is the most famous, and probably the best loved of them all. Lying close to Portland, this mountain can be seen from the western hills of that city, one of the most magical views in all of the Cascades. Right: a white water tapestry at Ramona Falls in the Mount Hood Wilderness on the slopes of the peak.

Legend has it that once, when a great sickness afflicted the Multnomah people, the medicine man informed them that the only way to eradicate the illness was for a maiden to throw herself from the cliff of Multnomah Falls (left) on the Columbia River – Oregon's highest falls. None came forward, but when the chief's daughter saw her lover fall ill, she sacrificed herself at this spot. Now, when a breeze blows through the falls a mist forms the shape of a woman, a sign that the Great Spirit accepted her martyrdom. Facing page: Oneonta Gorge on the Columbia River, Oregon.

Facing page: an uncluttered sky over Skagit Flats, an agricultural area near LaConner, northwest Washington. First settled in 1864, LaConner is Skagit County's oldest city. Right: Washington's Palouse farm country, some of the most fertile on the continent, particularly for wheat, peas and apples. Below: the Palouse River cuts a deep canyon between cliffs on its way south to join the Snake. The Palouse Indians wove their own legends about the Palouse and believed that a mythological "Big Beaver" gouged out the canyon walls and the falls.

Dead wood has a beauty all its own on the slopes of Mount Rainier, the highlight of Mount Rainier National Park in central Washington. The peak is a 14,410-foot-high dormant volcano with more glaciers on its slopes than any other mountain in the contiguous United States.

Over one-and-a-half million people visit Mount Rainier National Park (these pages) every year, enchanted by the beauty of this distinctive, broad-shouldered peak (below and facing page) and the unspoilt wilderness that surrounds it. Waterfalls (left) grace many of the hiking trails in Rainier's backcountry, where the hiking season is quite short – most trails are only snow-free from mid-July to mid-October. The most famous of these, the Wonderland Trail, comprises ninety-three miles of mountain passes, forests and meadows, and completely encircles the mountain. Another, less demanding, way to view the park's centerpiece is via the Mount Rainier Scenic Railroad on board a steam train from Elbe station.

Above: first light strikes the ridge of Crystal Mountain on the very edge of Mount Rainier National Park, part of the Cascade Range, Washington. South of the park Mount Adams (left) looms, a dormant volcano like its neighbors Mount Rainier and Mount St. Helens. Novice mountaineers often use Mount Adams as a first climb, since it is one of the easiest Northwest volcanic peaks to scale, despite its respectable height of 12, 276 feet, the south face being the easiest route up. Right: winter alpenglow and hemlocks at sunset in Park Butte, Washington.

The fleecy rows of clouds that form a mackerel sky are perfectly reflected in the still, cool waters of Upper Goose Lake, Washington.

Diablo Lake in North Cascades National Park, Washington. The lake lies on the North Cascades Scenic Highway. It owes its turquoise/emerald green color to mineral-rich glacial run-off from the peaks surrounding it; a color which is partly responsible for the lake's attraction for visitors, though the well-sited lodge nearby is also a draw. Above: breathtakingly beautiful Mount Shuksan. Though, at just over 8,000 feet, its summit is not as high as other peaks in the North Cascades, Mount Shuksan is the most frequently photographed for the beauty of its setting.

Facing page and right: Seattle, Washington's first city, which enjoys an enviable reputation as one of the nation's most desirable locations. Situated beside Puget Sound in the north of the state and backed by the majestic Cascade Range, Seattle has experienced phenomenal growth in the last half of this century. Much of this is due to the success of the nearby Boeing aircraft plant, which employs many thousands and forms the main industry in the region, but Seattle's reputation for clean air, friendly people, beautiful surroundings and justifiable civic pride is a considerable draw as well. Above: Deception Bridge connects the San Juan Islands – known as the jewels of Puget Sound – in northwest Washington.

Left: the somber greens of coniferous trees and the slate gray of the earth and rock provide the perfect foil for the reds and yellows of fall in northern Washington. Right: logs washed up on the beach at Anacortes, which lies at the tip of Fidalgo Island, the passageway to the San Juan Islands in Puget Sound, northwest Washington. Below: sunset on the Great Bend, the southernmost point of Hood Canal, which borders the Olympic Peninsula and the Cascades in northwest Washington.

The serrated silhouettes of conifers find their white counterparts in the ridges of the Olympic Mountains, which form the backbone of Olympic National Park, Washington.

Left: an Olympic Peninsula lake, and (below) the Hall of Mosses in Olympic National Park on the Pacific coast, both in Washington. The park receives the most rain of any spot in the conterminous United States and such a profusion of mosses, lichen and fungi are the result. Cars have been banned in Olympic National Park, which has been named a "World Heritage Park" by the United Nations for the diversity of its ecology. Overleaf: Mount Vernon, north of Seattle, Washington.